Latin

Latin

A Joyously Brief Introduction

Jon-David Hague

WESTBRAE LITERARY GROUP

Berkeley

2024

PARENTIBUS

Contents

About the Author and Acknowledgements

Jon-David Hague earned his PhD in Classical Studies at Boston University. He holds a BA from Luther College, where he double-majored in Latin and Greek. His early studies in Latin and Greek began at Captain Shreve High School, a public school in Shreveport, Louisiana, where he was born.

Hague's dissertation, *Presenting the Divine: Stagecraft and Politics in Aristophanes' "Birds"*, was completed under the guidance of Jeffrey Henderson, who generously reviewed the manuscript for this brief book and offered invaluable insights.

Donald Carne-Ross, Hague's mentor, enriched his education through reading the Greek Anthology, especially the works of Anyte. Hague also worked under Wolfgang Haase on the *Aufstieg und Niedergang der römischen Welt* and the *International Journal of the Classical Tradition*.

Special thanks are due to Sheri Childs, who first introduced him to Latin in his sophomore year of high school. Gratitude also goes to Erin Kehoe, Emily Beugelmans Cook, Dr. Brandon Cock, Jay Youngdhal, Joshua Greenbaum, and Lester Raww for their valuable suggestions. Additional appreciation is extended to Dickinson College's Classics Department for their excellent online Latin vocabulary lists.

Any merits of this book are due to the support and contributions of those mentioned here; all remaining flaws are solely the author's.

Introduction

The words "Latin" and "joy" don't often occur in the same sentence. That's a shame. Knowing some Latin can be joyous. The poetry of Lucretius, Catullus, Vergil, and Horace is worthy of that joy as is Cicero's intricate yet clear prose.

Dip into this book on any page, as each page was written to be self-contained.

In addition to learning the basics of the Latin language, you'll become familiar with the timeline for Latin literature, be able to read lines from real Latin, and perhaps even memorize some lines, which is encouraged. In the end, your English grammar and writing will be better too.

This book isn't meant to be a comprehensive Latin grammar. For thorough works, I give some recommendations near the end of this book. One resource of note, however, is the renowned Loeb Classical Library, which, in handsome, hand-held red volumes for Latin (and green for Greek), contains nearly all of ancient Latin and Greek literature with the ancient language on one side and English translation on the other.

There should be enough here in this book that you will be able to read real Latin and get the right meaning from it. This will entail feeling the Latin and imaging the meaning in your mind without English. **Id mihi faciendum est**. "It for me a doing thing is." That's the word-for-word meaning of that sentence but we'd translate that as "I have to do this." With practice, you can *learn* the vocabulary and grammar, but also *feel* the Latin.

English and Latin

English is an interesting mix of Latin, Romance languages ("Roman" languages are French, Spanish, Italian, Portuguese, and Romanian) and Germanic languages. In simplest terms:

- **Complex and Academic Words** often derive from Latin (and Greek) and Romance languages, reflecting the influence of classical education, science, medicine, and law.
- **Everyday Simple Words** typically come from Old English, a Germanic language, which provides the core vocabulary used in daily communication.

Latin has significantly shaped English vocabulary, especially from the influence of the Roman Empire, the Christian Church, and the Renaissance. About 40% of English words have Latin origins, particularly in scientific, technical, and academic contexts.

French, as a major Romance language, has contributed many words to English, and did so particularly after the Norman (French) Conquest of England in 1066. This includes legal, military, and cultural terminology. Nearly 30% of English words are derived from French.

The fundamental structure and most common, everyday words in English come from Old English, which is a Germanic language. This includes basic vocabulary like "house," "mother," "food," and "day."

Dates and Dating

I use BCE for dates before the birth of Jesus of Nazareth and CE for dates after. BCE stands for Before the Common Era and CE stands for Common Era.

For roughly 1600 years (44 BCE to around 1580 CE), Romans and Europe used the Julian calendar (a near accurate solar calendar), which Julius Caesar put forward and Rome started to use before his assassination in 44 BCE.

The Romans dated their years from the founding of Rome (753 BCE), their year 1. Scholars have called this **ab urbe condita**, "from when the city was built" or AUC. Ancient Romans might have noted that Caesar was assassinated in 710 AUC, our 44 BCE.

Today, to mark our years, some use BC (Before Christ) and AD which stands for Latin **anno domini** or "in the year of the lord/Jesus." Dionysius Exiguus, a scholar monk living in Rome sometime in the early 500s CE – not long after the fall of the Roman Empire in 476 CE – invented **anno domini** and calculated Jesus's birth at 753 years after the founding of Rome, which is our year 1.

Around 1580 CE, in Europe, the western Christian church adopted the Gregorian calendar (a more accurate solar calendar that accounted for the annual drift in the Julian calendar) and used Exiguus's year 1 to begin numbering years from the birth of Jesus of Nazareth. Today, much of the world uses the Gregorian calendar.

The Latin Authors We Can Read Today

In the 300s CE, there were over twenty public libraries in Rome that contained (we might assume) copies of most of what had been written and published in Latin. The very first public library was established by Gaius Asinius Pollio (a Roman of many talents) in 39 BCE. For much of antiquity, books were rolls  a person would unroll and reroll as they read the columns, which were typically ten inches tall with about thirty lines of text. Somewhere around the 300s CE, a book form we would recognize today became more common.

By the 500s CE, Rome had fallen to the Goths, Germanic peoples. Preserving Latin literature was not a priority for them. Earlier, during the 300s CE, Rome had become a Christian empire and as these non-Christian Goths gained dominance in 476 CE, the Christian Church and its monasteries were a refuge for works of Latin. Still, most of these works, maybe up to 90%, have not survived for a variety of reasons, not least of all because they were not Christian texts. Also, writing materials were scarce and expensive, so monks sometimes reused the rolls and books to copy Christian texts (this type of manuscript we call a palimpsest).

Within Classical Latin from 80 BCE to 20 CE, that 100 year period, there are roughly 20 or so surviving authors who are commonly read.

The *Apparatus Criticus* in Latin Texts

If you continue to learn Latin in earnest, you will likely buy a book prepared and edited by scholars that contains the Latin of an author you find interesting.

As you begin to read, you will notice something at the bottom of the page that looks like footnotes. That is called the *apparatus criticus*, which provides notes from the scholar who prepared the text about any variations that might exist for any line of Latin text on that page.

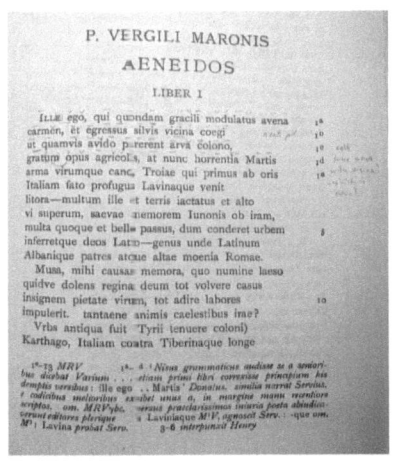

The job of the scholar preparing the text is to provide, after much scholarly work, what they understand to be the actual words the author used. There can be variations in the text because in all of antiquity – pick any text from either a Greek or Roman author – we have not one original copy or first edition. We only have hand copies of copies of copies over centuries, which are subject to error. This is true also of the Christian New Testament.

Therefore, a scholar must understand the genealogy (so to say) of the text from the non-existent original through all the copies to the text they construct and present to the reader. The *apparatus criticus* contains the notes for each line with variations, including conjectures from more recent scholars.

Old Latin: The Historical Scope

The history of Latin and its literature is also the history of Rome, which was founded in 753 BCE and fell in 476 CE, a span of over 1,200 years.

Early Latin is sometimes called Old Latin and comes mostly to us from inscriptions, or writings on objects that have survived like stones or pottery.

From 753 BCE to 509 BCE, Rome was a monarchy. The last Roman king, Tarquinius, was thrown out in 509 BCE after his son raped a noble-woman name

Lucretia, who committed suicide over the atrocity. The earliest account we have of this is from the Roman historian Livy, some 500 years later. But Lucretia has ever since been famous in no less than Dante, Chaucer, and Shakespeare to name a few. Her virtue, in stark contrast to the assault against her, represented a catalyst for change.

After the monarchy, a system was created in which two consuls, the highest office, were elected, each able to check the other's power by veto. This system, the Roman Republic, lasted nearly 500 years until 27 BCE when Augustus, Julius Caesar's heir, took complete rule and the Roman Empire began.

Old Latin spans this era from the founding until roughly 75 BCE, when Classical Latin finds prominence. But during this period of Old Latin, Latin's literary roots were established.

The Birth of Latin Literature

We know the precise date of the birth of Latin literature, which might seem odd. It's 240 BCE. After the first battle between the Romans and the Carthaginians of North Africa for the control of the Mediterranean world, called the First Punic War, which Rome won in 241 BCE, the Romans (the aediles to be precise, who were elected officials in charge of public festivals) added Greek tragedy and Greek comedy productions, in Latin, to their annual fall festival called the *ludi romani* (Roman games/entertainment/fun). That year was 240 BCE.

In winning the First Punic War, the Romans were establishing dominance in the Mediterranean where the Greeks had once held sway. Further, there had been enough high level people in Rome who had been influenced by the greatness of Greek literature and drama (and poetry) that these dramatic performances each year at the *ludi romani* became official.

There had been one person, a Greek slave to a noble Roman family, who had translated Greek tragedies and comedies, and even Homer, into Latin. His work sparked the beginning. Livius Andronicus, a Greek slave, who wrote original dramas in Latin, based on Greek models, and had them performed at the *ludi romani* in 240 BCE, is the originator of Latin literature.

Latin in Its Earliest Phase

The first Latin literature we have is comedies and tragedies written around the 240s BCE. There is also some poetry and prose from this era. This is also the era in which Rome wars against Carthage (modern day Tunisia in north Africa) for dominance in the Mediterranean and wins. The main authors of this period, roughly from 250 BCE to later 100s BCE, are:

Author	Dates	Genre	Famous for
Livius Andronicus	250s BCE	Drama and epic poetry	Originator of Latin literature
Gnaeus Naevius	240s BCE	Drama and epic poetry	Exiled for his comedy being too critical
Titus Maccius **Plautus**	220s BCE	Drama	A comedy called *Miles Gloriosus* (braggart soldier)
Quintus **Ennius**	170s BCE	Poetry	His epic poem *Annales* chronicling the history of Rome
Marcus Porcius **Cato**	150s BCE	Prose	*De Agri Cultura* (On the cultivation of the land)

Latin in Its Finest Stage

Many would say the most prestigious periods for Latin are the Ciceronian and Augustan eras, spanning roughly from the life of Caesar (80s BCE) to the death of Rome's first emperor, Augustus (14 CE). This is Classical Latin.

Author	Dates	Genre	Famous for
Gaius Julius **Caesar**	100 BCE to March 15, 44 BCE	Prose	Ending the Roman Republic as Dictator
Marcus Tullius **Cicero**	106-43	Prose	Arguably Rome's greatest statesman; also consul (in 63 BCE
Titus **Lucretius** Carus	99-55	Poetry	*De Rerum Natura*/*On the Nature of Things*. Epic Poem about Epicurean philosophy
Gaius Valerius **Catullus**	84-54	Poetry	Love poems; hugely influential on poets still today
Gaius Sallustius Crispus (**Sallust**)	86-35	History	Earliest historian writing in prose Latin
Titus Livius (**Livy**)	59-17 CE	History	First full history of Rome up to his own lifetime
Publius **Vergil**ius Maro	70 to 19 CE	Poetry	*Aeneid*, epic poem relating the origins of Rome
Quintus Horatius Flaccus (**Horace**)	65-8	Poetry	The lyric poems in his *Odes*
Publius Ovidius Naso (**Ovid**)	43-17CE	Poetry	Epic poem *Metamorphoses* relating the origins and nature of Rome, through myth

Latin After Augustus in the Roman Empire

Latin literature after Augustus, beginning with his successor Tiberius in 14 CE and continuing until the fall of Rome almost 500 years later, is often referred to as the Silver Age of Latin (up to roughly 200 CE) and, thereafter, Late Latin. While literary expression may have been less free during this time due to tyrannical emperors like Caligula and Nero, it still flourished. Here are some significant authors from this period who are still widely read today.

Author	Dates	Genre	Famous for
Lucius Annaeus **Seneca**	4 BCE - 65 CE	Tragedies; Letters/Essays; Philosophy	Senator; tutored Nero; forced into suicide
Gaius Plinius Secondus (**Pliny the Elder**)	23 - 79	Natural philosophy (all things nature)	Died saving friends in Mt Vesuvius eruption in 79; authored vast encyclopedia on nature
Gaius **Petronius** Arbiter	27 - 66	Satirical Novel	*The Satyricon*. Read the Arrowsmith translation
Marcus Annaeus **Lucan**us	39 - 65	Poetry	*Pharsalia*, epic poem about Caesar's civil war at the end of the Republic
Marcus Valerius Martialis (**Martial**)	40 - 104	Poetry	Epigrams
Publius (?) Cornelius **Tacitus**	56 - 120	History	*Annales* and *Historiae* documenting the early Roman emperors
Apuleius	120s to 180	Novel	Born in present-day Algeria; authored *The Golden Ass*

Latin Near the End
and After the Fall of the Roman Empire

The era from the fall of Rome (476 CE) to the European Renaissance is called the Middle Ages, which ends around the 1450s CE. Latin during this time sees the birth of Christian literature notably **Augustine** of Hippo (354 to 430 from Numidia in North Africa) and his *De Civitate Dei* and **Jerome** (340s to 420 from the Dalmatian coast east of Italy across the Adriatic) who first translated the Christian Greek New Testament into Latin. In Northumbria, modern Northern England, the Venerable **Bede** (Venerabilis Beda about 700 CE or so) writes in Latin perhaps the first history of England including its Christian church history.

Later Renaissance Latin sees Descartes's philosophy, Linnaeus's many categorizations of our biological world (Latin names for plants and animals we still use today) and even Sir Isaac Newton and his *Philosophiae Naturalis Principia Mathematica/Mathematical Principles of Natural Philosophy*, in which Newton presents his laws of motion and gravity.

With the establishment of Latin as a common language of both the Christian Church and the European scientific community, Latin was set to endure as a written language (if not a spoken one) to this day.

Using a Latin Dictionary

The extent and effectiveness of your use of a Latin dictionary will correlate to your ability to read Latin.

Latin dictionaries will list nouns in their subject cases and verbs in their "I" person in the present tense. So the verb for "to love" you'll find under **amo**. Right next to **amo**/I love, dictionaries will give the infinitive form or **amare**. If it's an irregular verb that doesn't follow the regular pattern of the four types of Latin verbs, you'll also find the perfect and past perfect forms (**fero, ferre, tuli, latus**, "to carry" something).

Dictionaries will give the masculine, feminine, and neuter endings of adjectives. For nouns, you will get the nominative (subject) case and the genitive (possessive) case, which helps you know which of the five different types of Latin nouns it is.

When you use a dictionary, use two tactics. First, when you are trying to find a word from Latin you are reading, look for that exact word. If it's not listed, look around that area for similar words. Unless the word you are looking for is irregular (**tuli** for example you'll find under **fero**), a little sleuthing on the page will yield results. Second, be a reader of the dictionary! When you are looking up a word, read lots of entries nearby. You'll see many words are interrelated.

Pronunciation

English mostly has the same alphabet as Latin, but Latin didn't have a *j* (invented later in the 1500s CE) or a *w* (invented likely in the 600s or late 700s CE during the reign of Charlemange from Germanic *u*'s put together) and there was no *u* (only regularly used later in 1500s like *j*) because the letter *v* stood for both the *u* sound and the *w* sound (see below).

Vowels

ā "ah" (the line over the vowel, a macron, indicates it's long)

a "about"

ē "say"

e "let"

ī "eek"

i "in"

ō long like "own"

o short like "on"

ū long as in "attitude"

u short as in "book"

Vowel combinations (diphthongs)

ae "eye"

au "ouch"

ei "hay"

eu [ey oo]

oe "oil"

ui "ruin"

Consonants

c always hard

g always hard

i also a consonant like y in "you"

r trilled or rolled

v like w (probably started to sound like v during the early Roman Empire)

x like x in "dixon

Emphasis on Syllables

Latin is not hard to read aloud and is quite beautiful in a rugged way that can also be tender.

- Each syllable is pronounced. So, **ventus** (wind) is **VENtus. Fugio** (I escape) is **FUgio**.
- If you see two consonants together, the vowel before it in that syllable gets the emphasis. **Parentes** (parents - note the two consonants underlined) is **parENtes**.
- Long vowels get emphasis too. **Amāre** (to love) is **amARe**. Latin texts often do not give you long lines (macrons) over vowels. But your Latin dictionary will.

Here is the opening to a letter Seneca (an author of the Silver Age of Latin during the early Roman Empire) wrote to his friend Lucilius (from Pompeii) about the importance of not wasting your time. You can use this to practice reading aloud:

Ita fac, mi Lucili: vindica te tibi, et tempus, quod adhuc aut auferebatur aut subripiebatur aut excidebat, collige et serva. Persuade tibi hoc sic esse ut scribo: quaedam tempora eripiuntur nobis, quaedam subducuntur, quaedam effluunt. Turpissima tamen est iactura quae per neglegentiam fit. Et si volueris adtendere, magna pars vitae elabitur male agentibus, maxima nihil agentibus, tota vita aliud agentibus.

Word Order (Syntax) in Latin

In English sentences, meaning is derived from the word arrangement or syntax. For example, "Chris loves Pat" (does Pat love Chris?) is different from "Pat loves Chris" (does Chris love Pat?).

In Latin, the order of words can change while retaining the same basic meaning, though the emphasis might differ. For instance, **Claudia Julium amat** and **Julium Claudia amat** both mean "Claudia loves Julius." The word order is different, but the fundamental meaning remains the same, with a slight shift in emphasis based on which word comes first.

However, there are some general patterns for prose (poetry, like poetry in English, can break the rules):

1) Verbs like to be placed at the end (except the "to be" verb **sum, esse, fui, futurum** which can even be omitted: **usus magister est optimus** means "experience is the best teacher;" **nemo malus felix** means "no one who is bad is happy").
2) Subject nouns like to be placed early on.
3) Adjectives like to follow nouns.
4) Object and indirect object nouns like to be placed before the verb: **Claudia <u>litteram</u> legit**, "Claudia is reading a letter." **Claudia litteram <u>Julio</u> dedit**, "Claudia gave a letter to Julius" or "Claudia gave Julius a letter."
5) Adverbs like to be placed before the verb they modify.

Latin is an Inflected Language

My college Latin (and Greek) professor, William C. Kurth, said about Latin: "By their endings you will know them." The endings of Latin words help you understand what the sentence means. That is what an inflected language is. English, e.g., is only a mildly inflected language. My teacher's saying, I realized years later, was in fact from this Latin phrase: **a fructibus eorum cognoscetis eos**. "By their fruits you will know them" which Matthew, a disciple of Jesus of Nazareth, and biographer, has Jesus say about false prophets. That Latin is from the translation of the Greek New Testament that Jerome (called Hieronymus in Latin), an early Christian theologian, made in the 380s CE.

- **a** = preposition meaning by or from
- **fructibus** = a noun meaning fruits (i.e./id est the results of actions); the -ibus endings tells us it's plural and in the dative or ablative case
- **eorum** = a demonstrative adjective meaning they/them and the -orum ending tells us its plural and in the possessive case "of"
- **cognoscetis** = a verb that means to know and the -etis ending tells us it's future (the "e" in -etis) and that it's "you all" or you plural (the -tis ending)
- **eos** = that demonstrative adjective again meaning this/that/those. The -os ending tells us it's plural in the object case (them).
- And so the endings tell us what the sentence means. "**a**/from **fructibus**/fruits **eorum**/of them **cognoscetis**/know will you **eos**/them". It is important to pay attention to endings.

Gender

Nouns and adjectives can be masculine, feminine, or neuter. This is strange to native English speakers but not to speakers of Spanish, Italian, French, or German. Importantly, if a noun is masculine, the adjective that modifies it will be masculine, et cetera (etc.).

The word for man in Latin is **vir** and it's a masculine noun. The word for woman is **femina** and it's a feminine noun. The word for tree is **arbor** and it's a feminine noun. The first two seem logical but gender and sex (biological) don't always correspond. Even amongst languages there are differences: **sol** (sun) is a masculine noun in Latin but in German die Sonne is a feminine noun. Why?

There are some interesting explanations as to how gender arose for nouns and adjectives. A striking one is that early humans, as language was developing, would personify the physical world around them in relation to their social community both past and present. Think of the wonder and terror we must have had about the world around us from trees to sunrises and the moon not to mention the dangers of storms and predators. All these could have had word origins from us personifying them. The powerful storm was like a great grandmother or matriarch. In Latin storm is **tempestas**, a feminine noun.

There may be a connection between the stories we told ourselves – our oral histories or myths and stories about humans and super humans (gods) – and the words we needed to express and understand both the natural world around us and what we had learned from our ancestors. (See Ernst Cassirer's *Language and Myth*.)

Parts of Speech in Latin

In Latin, the endings of nouns, pronouns, adjectives, and verbs change in order to change the meaning of a sentence or clause. That's important to remember.

Knowing the parts of speech in Latin helps us understand the inflected nature of Latin. There are seven parts of speech to bear in mind. Think of them in the context of a movie:

1. **Nouns**: The main characters in a sentence. They can play various roles - as heroes (subjects), recipients (objects), or even the setting (place nouns).

2. **Adjectives**: The costumes and makeup for the characters (nouns). They add detail, color, and depth, helping to paint a more vivid picture of the nouns they describe.

3. **Pronouns**: The stand-ins or stunt doubles for nouns. They step in to avoid repetition, keeping the narrative (sentence) smooth and focused without losing the essence of who or what they are representing.

4. **Verbs**: The action sequences of a sentence. Just like in a movie, where action drives the plot forward, verbs propel a sentence, showing what the nouns (characters) are doing or what is happening to them.

5. **Adverbs)**: The special effects in a film. They modify verbs, adjectives, or other adverbs, adding nuance, intensity, or manner to the actions or descriptions.

6. **Prepositions (prep.)**: The directors of the sentence. They set the scene and direction. They help position the nouns in relation to each other, establishing the where, when, and how.

7. **Conjunctions (conj.)**: The scriptwriters, linking words, phrases, or clauses. They are responsible for the cohesion and flow of the sentence, connecting parts to tell a coherent and comprehensive story.

Nouns

Latin has five different kinds of nouns (*declensions*) that can have different endings on the words to denote the role of the word in the sentence. Here are examples of the five kinds:

1. **terra** (land); **vita** (life)
2. **animus** (mind, spirit); **deus** (god)
3. **tex** (king); **pars** (part); **pater** (father)
4. **manus** (hand); **domus** (house, home)
5. **res** (thing); **dies** (day)

Nouns in Latin change their endings to have a specific meaning in a sentence. The different endings we call *cases*. There are different endings (usually) for singular and plural nouns in each case. Here are the cases in Latin. Think of them in the context of a movie.

1. **Nominative (nom.)**: As the main actor, the nominative case or subject case, indicates the subject of the sentence – the main character or focus of the action.
2. **Genitive (gen.)**: This is a possessive label or a signature on an artwork. It shows ownership, origin, or association.
3. **Dative (dat.)**: This case, the indirect case, is like an outstretched hand, offering or receiving something. It's used for the indirect object in a sentence, representing the entity to whom or for whom something is given, shown, or done.
4. **Accusative (acc.)**: This can be visualized as a direct path or a target. The object case. It's used for the direct object of a sentence, pointing directly to the person, place, or thing that is directly affected by the action of the verb, much like a target is the intended point of impact.
5. **Ablative (abl.)**: Think of the ablative case as a set of tools or instruments. It's often used to express means, manner, or cause. It can also indicate separation or movement from something.
6. **Vocative (voc.)**: The vocative case is like a direct call or shout-out in a crowd. It's used for direct address, when you are speaking to someone directly, as if calling their name to grab their attention in a conversation or a speech.

Endings of the Five Kinds of Latin Nouns

5 types of nouns	Frequency	1	2		3		4		5
Singl.		*f*	*m*	*n*	*m/f*	*n*	*m*	*n*	*f*
Nom.	23%	-a	-us	-um	*varia*	*varia*	-us	-ū	-ēs
Gen.	14%	-ae	-ī	-ī	-is	-is	-ūs	-ūs	-ei
Dat.	5%	-ae	-ō	-ō	-ī	-ī	-ui	-ū	-ei
Acc.	32%	-am	-um	-um	-em	*same as nom.*	-um	-ū	-em
Abl.	26%	-ā	-ō	-ō	-e	-e	-ū	-ū	-e
Pl.									
Nom.		-ae	-ī	-a	-ēs	-a (-ia)	-ūs	-ua	-ēs
Gen.		-ārum	-ōrum	-ōrum	-um	-um (-ium)	-uum	-uum	-erum
Dat.		-īs	-īs	-īs	-ibus	-ibus	-ibus	-ibus	-ebus
Acc.		-ās	-ōs	-a	-ēs	-a (-ia)	-ūs	-ua	-ēs
Abl.		-īs	-īs	-īs	-ibus	-ibus	-ibus	-ibus	-ebus
Frequency		22%	24%		52%		1%		0.7%

Notice the frequency of both the *declensions*/kinds of nouns (that very bottom row) and the *cases* (top of second column for both singular and plural). Roughly half of the nouns you'll encounter when you read Latin will be third declension nouns. **rex** (king); **pars** (part); **pater** (father); **corpus** (body), **urbs** (city) are some of the most common third declension nouns.

f=feminine; m=masculine; n=neuter
Nom.=Nominative; Gen.=Genitive; Dat.=Dative; Acc =Accusative; Abl =Ablative
Singl. = Singular; Pl. = Plural

Adjectives

Adjectives describe nouns. In order to do this, Latin adjectives follow the case and gender of the noun they describe.

3 types of adjectives	1 and 2			3	
Singular	*m*	*f*	*n*	*m/f*	*n*
Nominative	-us	-a	-um	-is	-e
Genitive	-ī	-ae	-ī	-is	-is
Dative	-ō	-ae	-ō	-ī	-ī
Accusative	-um	-am	-um	-em	-e
Ablative	-ō	-ā	-ō	-ī	-ī
Plural					
Nominative	-ī	-ae	-a	-ēs	-ia
Genitive	ōrum	-ārum	-ōrum	-ium	-ium
Dative	-īs	-īs	-īs	-ibus	-ibus
Accusative	-ōs	-ās	-a	-ēs	-ia
Ablative	-īs	-īs	-īs	-ibus	-ibus

Any of the five kinds of nouns can go with any of the three kinds of adjectives: **ventus levis** (light wind) or **ventus magnus** (great wind).

f=feminine; m=masculine; n=neuter

Comparative Adjectives

Regular Comparative Adjectives

Degree	Magnus	Fortis	Bonus	Malus	Parvus
Positive *(m/f/n)*	Magnus (big/great)	Fortis (strong)	Bonus (good)	Malus (bad)	Parvus (small)
Comparative *(m/f)*	Maior (bigger/greater)	Fortior (stronger)	Melior (better)	Peior (worse)	Minor (smaller)
Comparative *(n)*	Maius (bigger/greater)	Fortius (stronger)	Melius (better)	Peius (worse)	Minus (smaller)
Superlative *(m/f/n)*	Maximus (biggest/greatest)	Fortissimus (strongest)	Optimus (best)	Pessimus (worst)	Minimus (smallest)

Irregular Comparative Adjectives

Degree	Bonus	Malus	Magnus	Parvus	Multus	Paucus
Positive *(m/f/n)*	Bonus (good)	Malus (bad)	Magnus (great)	Parvus (small)	Multus (many)	Paucus (few)
Comparative *(m/f)*	Melior (better)	Peior (worse)	Maior (greater)	Minor (smaller)	Pluris (more)	Paucior (fewer)
Comparative *(n)*	Melius (better)	Peius (worse)	Maius (greater)	Minus (smaller)	Pluris (more)	Paucius (fewer)
Superlative *(m/f/n)*	Optimus (best)	Pessimus (worst)	Maximus (greatest)	Minimus (smallest)	Plurimus (most)	Paucissimus (fewest)

Quam or a noun in the ablative case serves as "than" in comparisons. In Sulpicia's poem we see

> tandem venit amor, qualem texisse pudori
> **quam** nudasse alicui sit mihi fama **magis**.

Love has finally come, the kind that would bring *more* rumor for me if I hid it in shame *than* reveal it to someone.

f=feminine; m=masculine; n=neuter

Pronouns

Type	The Latin Pronouns	
Personal	ego/me tu/te nos vos	I, me you we you all
Possessive	meus, mea, meum tuus, tua, tuum suus, sua, suum noster, nostra, nostrum vester, vestra, vestrum	my your his, her, its, their own our your pl.
Demonstrative	hic, haec, hoc ille, illa, illud iste, ista, istud is, ea, id ei, eae, ea	this, these that, those that, those he, she, it they
Relative	qui, quae, quod	who, which
Interrogative	quis, quid qui, quae, quae	who? what? *singl.* which? what? *pl.*
Reflexive	se, sui	himself, herself, itself, themselves
Indefinite	quidam, quaedam, quidam a certain one/thing quisque, quaeque, quodque each, every	

Verbs

There are four conjugations (or types) of verbs. The *person* (I, you, she, he, it, we, you all, and they) is known from the ending of the verb. Most verbs have endings as in this chart:

Person	Active	Passive
I	-o, -m	-r
you	-s	-ris
she, he, it	-t	-tur
we	-mus	-mur
you all	-tis	-mini
they	-nt	-ntur

Of the four types, verbs can be *active* like **matrem amo** "I love my mom" or *passive* like **mater ab filio amatur** "A mom is loved by her son." Some verbs can be *transitive* with an object (noun or verb) like **edere volo** "I want to eat" or *intransitive* like **volo** by itself with no object, "I am willing."

Verbs can represent time in six ways: 1) the *present*, like **do** "I give"; 2) the *continuous past*, like **desiderabam** "I used to want" or **stabam** "I was standing"; 3) the *perfect past*, like **erravi** "I got it wrong" or **dubitavi** "I hesitated"; 4) the *past perfect*, like **vocaveram** "I had called"; 5) the *future*, like **desiderabo** "I will want"; 6) the *future past*, like **desideravero** "I will have wanted."

Verbs have one of three *moods*: 1) *indicative* – statement of what is; 2) *subjunctive* – what could or might happen, like **vocem** "I could call" or "I may call"; 3) *imperative* – when you give an order, like **me ama**, "love me!"

Understanding Changes in Verb Forms

The four conjugations of verbs have different forms to indicate past, present, or future as well as verb mood and voice.

	amo, -are, -avi, -atus	deleo, -ēre, -evi, -etus	emo, -ere, -ēmi, emptus	audio, -īre, -ivi, -itus
Indicative active and passive	*1*	*2*	*3*	*4*
Present (am, is)	-a-	-e-	-i-	-i-
Continuous Past (was)	-ba-	-ba-	-ba-	-ba-
Past (have)	-av-	-ev-	*	-iv-
Past of the Past (had)	-avera-	-evera-	-era-	-ivera-
Future (will)	-bo, -bi-	-bo, -bi-	-a-, -ē-	-ia-/ie-
Future Past (will have)	-avero/-i-	-evero/-i-	-ero/-i-	-ivero/-i-
Subjunctive active and passive	*1*	*2*	*3*	*4*
Present (may)	-e-	-a-	-a-	-a-
Continuous Past (might)	-are-	-ēre-	-ere-	-ire-
Past (may have)	-averi-	-ēveri-	-eri-	-iveri-
Past of the Past (might have)	-avisse-	-ēvisse-	-isse-	-ivisse-
Imperative active	*1*	*2*	*3*	*4*
Present (you)	-a	-ē	-e	-i
Present (you all)	-ate	-ēte	-ite	-ite
Future (you or he/she/it)	-amato	-eto	-ito	-ito
Future (you all)	-amtote	-etote	-itote	-itote
Future (they)	-amanto	-ento	-unto	-iunto
Imperative passive	*1*	*2*	*3*	*4*
Present (you)	-āre	-ēre	-ere	-ire
Present (you all)	-mini	-mini	-mini	-mini
Future (you or he/she/it)	-tor	-tor	-itor	-itor
Future (they)	-ntor	-ntor	-ntor	-iuntor

How to Translate the Person and Tense of Verbs

No matter the kind of verb, of the four kinds, you can translate the *voice*, the *mood*, and the *tense* like this:

ACTIVE	Indicative	Subjunctive	Imperative
Present	I love; I am loving	I may love	love! (you or you all)
Continuous Past (Imperfect)	I was loving; I used to love	I might love	*Doesn't exist*
Final Past (Perfect)	I have loved	I may have loved	*Doesn't exist*
Past of the Past (Pluperfect)	I had loved	I might have loved	*Doesn't exist*
Future	I will love; I will be loving	*Doesn't exist*	no English equivalent (in the future, love!)
Future Past (Future Perfect)	I will have loved	*Doesn't exist*	*Doesn't exist*
PASSIVE	Indicative	Subjunctive	Imperative
Present	I am loved	I may be loved	be loved! (you or you all)
Continuous Past (Imperfect)	I was being loved	I might be loved	*Doesn't exist*
Final Past (Perfect)	I have been loved	I may have been loved	*Doesn't exist*
Past of the Past (Pluperfect)	I had been loved	I might have been loved	*Doesn't exist*
Future	I will be loved	*Doesn't exist*	no English equivalent (in the future, be loved!)
Future Past (Future Perfect)	I will have been loved	*Doesn't exist*	*Doesn't exist*

Irregular Verbs

In English, *regular verbs* follow a regular pattern: I want; I wanted; I have wanted; I use; I used; I have used; I look; I looked; I have looked. *Irregular verbs* don't: I go; I went; I have gone; I see; I saw; I have seen.

In Latin, it's the same. Here is a list of the five most common:

eo	ire	ii or ivi	itus
I go	to go	I have gone	a person who has gone
fero	**ferre**	**tuli**	**latus**
I bear or I carry	to bear or to carry	I have born or I have carried	has been born or carried
fio	**fieri**	*n/a*	**factus sum**
I become, I happen	to become, to happen		I have become
possum	**posse**	**potui**	*n/a*
I am able to	to be able to	I have been able	
sum	**esse**	**fui**	**futurus**
I am	to be	I have been	about to be
volo	**velle**	**volui**	*n/a*
I wish or I am willing	to wish or to be willing	I have wished or I have been willing	

Deponent Verbs

These verb types look like passive verbs but have active verb meanings. Here are the most common.

Deponent Verb	Definition
arbitror, arbitrārī, arbitrātus sum	consider, think
cōnfiteor, cōnfitērī, cōnfessus sum	admit, confess
cōnor, cōnārī, cōnātus sum	try, attempt
cōnsequor, consequī, consecūtus sum	follow up, overtake
ēgredior, ēgredī, ēgressus sum	stride out, depart
experior, experīrī, expertus sum	try thoroughly
fateor, fatērī, fassus sum	admit, confess; profess, declare
for, fārī, fātus sum	report, say
fruor, fruī, frūctus sum	enjoy the produce of, profit by, use (+ abl.)
hortor, hortārī, hortātus sum	urge strongly, advise
ingredior, ingredī, ingressus sum:	step in, enter
īrāscor, īrāscī, īrātus sum	grow angry

loquor, loquī, locūtus sum	speak, talk
mīror, mīrārī, mīrātus sum	wonder at, marvel at (+ acc.)
morior, morī, mortuus sum	die
moror, morārī, morātus sum	delay
nāscor, nāscī, nātus sum	be born
orior, orīrī, ortus sum	arise, begin
patior, patī, passus sum	permit, endure
precor, preārī, precātus sum	pray, invoke
proficīscor, proficīscī, profectus sum	set forth, go
queror, querī, questus sum	complain of, lament
reor, rērī, rātus sum	think, imagine, suppose
sequor, sequī, secūtus sum	follow
ūtor, ūtī, ūsus sum	use, consume, employ (+ abl.)
vereor, verērī, veritus sum	fear, stand in awe of

Adverbs

Adverb	Definition
adhūc	thus far, to this point
bene	well
deinde/dein	then, next
diū	for a long time
etiam	also, even
haud	not
hīc	here; hinc = from here
hūc	to this place
iam	now; already
illīc	at that place, there
inde	from there, from then
ita	thus, so
longē	far, far off
magis	more
modo	just, just now; modo ... modo: at one moment ... at another
ne	interrogative particle attached to the emphatic word
nōn	not
numquam	never
nunc	now
parum	too little
prīmum	at first, firstly
procul	at a distance
quam	how?; (after comparative) than
quidem	certainly, at least
quō	for which reason; to or in what place
saepe	often
satis, sat	enough, sufficiently
semper	always, ever
sīc	in this manner, thus; sīc ... ut: in the same way as
simul	at the same time
tam	so, so much
tamquam	so as, just as
tantum, tantummodo	only
tot	so many
tum or tunc	then
ubi	where, when
unde	from where
ut, utī	as (+ indic.); with the result that (+ subj.)
vērō	in fact, without doubt
vix	scarcely

Prepositions

These are single words that "go with" nouns to help give extra meaning regarding physical or temporal relation.

Preposition	Definition and case needed for noun
ā, ab, abs	from, by (+ abl.)
ad	to, up to, towards (+ acc.)
ante	before, in front of (+ acc.)
apud	near, in the presence of (+ acc.)
circā	around (+ acc.)
contrā	against, opposite (+ acc.)
cum	with (+ abl.)
dē	down from, about, concerning (+ abl.)
ex, ē	out of, from (+ abl.)
in	in, on (+ abl.); into, onto (+ acc)
inter	between, among; during (+ acc.)
intrā	within (+ acc.)
ob	against, on account of (+acc)
per	through (+ acc.)
post	after (+ acc.)
praeter	by, along, past; besides, except (+ acc.)
prō	for, on behalf of, in proportion to (+ abl.)
prope	near (+ acc.)
propter	because of (+ acc.)
sine	without (+ abl.)
sub	under, close to (+ acc. or abl.)
suprā	above (+ acc.)
ultrā	beyond (+ acc.)

Conjunctions

Conj.	Definitions
ac	and, and also
an	or (in questions)
antequam	before
at	but, but yet
atque	and, as well as
aut	or
autem	moreover, but, however
cum	when, since, although
dōnec	until
dum	while (+ indic.); until (+ subj.); provided that (+ subj.)
enim	for, indeed
ergō	therefore
et	and
igitur	therefore
itaque	and so, therefore
licet	even though
nam or namque	for, indeed, really
nē	lest, that not
nec	and not, nor; nec ... nec, neither ... nor;
neque	and not, nor; neque ... neque, neither ... nor
nisi, nī	if not, unless
postquam	after
quamquam	however, although
que	and (added at end of word)
quia	because
quōmodo	in what way, how?
quoniam	since, seeing that
quoque	also, too
sed	but
seu	whether; seu ... seu: whether ... or → sīve
sī	if
sīve	whether; sīve ... sīve: whether ... or
tamen	nevertheless, still
uterque, utraque, utrumque	each of two
utrum	whether; utrum ... an: whether ... or
ve	or (postpositive enclitic)
vel	or else, or; even; vel ... vel: either ... or

Infinitives

An infinitive is like a verbal noun. It can be the *subject* of the sentence as in "to sing/singing is fun" or **iucundum canere**. It can be the *object* of a verb as in "I want to sing" or **canere volo**. You can also find the infinitive in *indirect speech* as in Seneca: **Persuade tibi hoc sic esse** (to be) **ut scribo**, "Persuade yourself *that* this is just like I'm writing [it here]".

Tense and Voice	1 amāre	2 vidēre	3 legere	4 audīre
Present Active	**amāre** (to love)	**vidēre** (to see)	**legere** (to read)	**audīre** (to hear)
Present Passive	**amārī** (to be loved)	**vidērī** (to be seen)	**legī** (to be read)	**audīrī** (to be heard)
Perfect Active	**amāvisse** (to have loved)	**vīdisse** (to have seen)	**lēgisse** (to have read)	**audīvisse** (to have heard)
Perfect Passive	**amātus esse** (to have been loved)	**vīsus esse** (to have been seen)	**lectus esse** (to have been read)	**audītus esse** (to have been heard)
Future Active	**amātūrus esse** (to be about to love)	**vīsūrus esse** (to be about to see)	**lēctūrus esse** (to be about to read)	**audītūrus esse** (to be about to hear)
Future Passive	**amātus īrī** (to be about to be loved)	**vīsus īrī** (to be about to be seen)	**lectus īrī** (to be about to be read)	**audītus īrī** (to be about to be heard)
Future Perfect Passive	**amātus fore** (to have been about to be loved)	**vīsus fore** (to have been about to be seen)	**lectus fore** (to have been about to be read)	**audītus fore** (to have been about to be heard)

Gerunds

Like infinitives, gerunds are verbal nouns. Unlike infinitives, gerunds are not the subject of a sentence.

You will recognize a gerund by *-nd-* in the word before the case ending (easy to remember because the word gerund ends in -nd).

For example:

ars scribendi is "the art of writing" where **scribendi** is a gerund genitive singular form of the verb **scribo, scribere**.

legendo discimus means "we learn by reading" where **legendo** is the ablative singular gerund of the verb **lego, legere**.

In Cicero we see the phrase **hic munitissimus habendi senatus locus** or "the most guarded place here of holding/having the senatus (object case)", where **habendi** is a gerund from **habeo, habere**. Notice too the nice sandwich of **munitissimus...locus**.

The preposition **ad** plus the gerund in singular neuter form is common to express purpose or result:

ad discendum venimus means "we came to learn" or "we came in order to learn" or "we came for the learning."

If you understand that **ad** as a preposition can mean motion toward or directed at/toward something, **ad discendum** intuitively makes sense.

Gerundives

These are verbal adjectives. In essence you can't tell the difference between gerunds and gerundives except in use. The -nd- plus case endings also distinguish the gerundive like the gerund.

But like adjectives, gerundives need to match the noun they modify.

liber legendus, a "reading book," means "a book that is to be read" or "a book that must be read." Note the meaning of *necessity* here.

liber mihi legendus est means "it is a reading book for me" or "I have to read this book."

Sometimes the noun in a sentence with a gerundive is missing or implied:

moriendum est means something/it "is a dying thing" (from the deponent verb **morior** I am dying) but we'd translate this as "death is necessary" or "death is inevitable."

Supines

Like infinitives, gerunds, and gerundives, supines are noun-like and also have verb qualities. As verbal nouns, they only occur in the accusative case with -**tum** as the ending or the ablative case with -**tu** as the ending. Supines have two special uses.

First, the supine form of -**tum** indicates *purpose* and is used with verbs of motion.

> **ad Caesarem gratulatum convenerunt** or "they went to Caesar to congratulate" or "they went to congratulate Caesar."

The second kind of supine is with certain adjectives like easy/**facile** or hard/**difficile**. The -**tu** ending as a verbal noun literally translates as "with respect to the *verb+ing*" or "in the *verb+ing*."

> **facile lectu** means "easy with respect to the reading" or "easy to read"

> **mirabile visu** means "wonderful with respect to the seeing" or "wonderful to see"

> **Id dictu quam re facilius est** means "it with respect to the saying than the thing easier is" or "easier said than done"

Supinus in Latin means "lying on the back." **Supinus erat** "He was supine" means he was lying on his back (dormant). Supines in Latin don't change; they end either -**tu** or -**tum**, dormant – just lying there.

Participles

Latin uses participles where English might use a clause or phrase. In English we recognize the present participle by the -ing ending. "Walking down the street the other day, I ran into my friend." But "I ran into my friend the other day walking down the street" could have two meanings. Who was walking down the street? Me or my friend? In Latin the particle will match the noun so there is no confusion.

We recognize the *present participle* in Latin by the -**ns** and -**nt**- endings. **Amans** means someone who is loving. **Amantes** mean people who are loving.

In Seneca's letters we see "**male agentibus**" which means "for those who are doing poorly" or "the doing poorly ones."

There is also the *past participle* which we recognize in English by the -ed ending. "Frustrated she couldn't find parking, Pam just went back home." "Pam went home because she was frustrated she couldn't find parking." In Latin, the -**t**- plus ending helps us recognize the past participle. Like **amata** (she who was loved) or **emptum** (a thing that was bought).

liber lectus means "the book that was read."

libro lecto is a common form in the ablative case, called the *ablative absolute*, meaning "with the book having been read." As a phrase in English we can translate it like this, "After the book was read..."or "after s/he read the book."

36

Conditional Sentences

Type	Time Frame	Condition Reality	If Clause (Condition)	Main Clause (Result)	Example
Simple Fact (Real)	Present	Likely/Possible	Si + indicative	Indicative	**Si venis, laetus sum** (If you come, I am happy)
Simple Fact (Real)	Past	Likely/Possible	Si + indicative	Indicative	**Si venisti, laetus eram** (If you came, I was happy)
Future More Vivid (Real)	Future	Likely	Si + future indicative	Future indicative	**Si venies, laetus ero** (If you will come, I will be happy)
Present Contrary-to-Fact	Present	Unreal/Not True	Si + imperfect subjunctive	Imperfect subjunctive	**Si venires, laetus essem** (If you were to come, I would be happy)
Past Contrary-to-Fact	Past	Unreal/Did Not Happen	Si + pluperfect subjunctive	Pluperfect subjunctive	**Si venisses, laetus fuissem** (If you had come, I would have been happy)
Future Less Vivid (Potential)	Future	Hypothetical	Si + present subjunctive	Present subjunctive or future indicative	**Si veniat, laetus sim** (If he should come, I would be happy)

Numbers

Cardinal Numbers

1 - Unus, Una, Unum (one)
2 - Duo, Duae, Duo (two)
3 - Tres, Tria (three)
4 - Quattuor (four)
5 - Quinque (five)
6 - Sex (six)
7 - Septem (seven)
8 - Octo (eight)
9 - Novem (nine)
10 - Decem (ten)
11 - Undecim (eleven)
12 - Duodecim (twelve)
13 - Trecenti (thirteen)
14 - Quattuordecim (fourteen)
15 - Quindecim (fifteen)
16 - Sedecim (sixteen)
17 - Septendecim (seventeen)
18 - Duodeviginti (eighteen)
19 - Undeviginti (nineteen)
20 - Viginti (twenty)

Ordinal Numbers

1st - Primus, Prima, Primum (first)
2nd - Secundus, Secunda, Secundum (second)
3rd - Tertius, Tertia, Tertium (third)
4th - Quartus, Quarta, Quartum (fourth)
5th - Quintus, Quinta, Quintum (fifth)
6th - Sextus, Sexta, Sextum (sixth)
7th - Septimus, Septima, Septimum (seventh)
8th - Octavus, Octava, Octavum (eighth)
9th - Nonus, Nona, Nonum (ninth)
10th - Decimus, Decima, Decimum (tenth)
11th - Undecimus, Undecima, Undecimum (eleventh)
12th - Duodecimus, Duodecima, Duodecimum (twelfth)
13th - Tertius Decimus (thirteenth)
14th - Quartus Decimus (fourteenth)
15th - Quintus Decimus (fifteenth)
16th - Sextus Decimus (sixteenth)
17th - Septimus Decimus (seventeenth)
18th - Duodevicesimus (eighteenth)
19th - Undevicesimus (nineteenth)
20th - Vicesimus, Vicesima, Vicesimum (twentieth)

Letters Used for Numbers

I = 1 or first
V = 5 or fifth (VI = 6 but IV = 4 or 1 minus 5)
X = 10 or tenth (XI = 11 but IX = 9 or 1 minus 10)
L = 50 or fiftieth
C = 100 or one-hundredth
D = 500 or five-hundredth
M = 1000 or one-thousandth

MMXXIV = 2024
MCMLXXXIV = 1984
(1000+(100-1000)+50+30+4)

Latin Poetic Meter

Latin poets used syllable stress of long vowels and short. Long syllables (–) can be caused by either a long vowel, a diphthong, or a short vowel followed by two or more consonants. Short syllables (⏑) have a short vowel not followed by more than one consonant. Latin verse is composed of units called "feet," which are combinations of long and short syllables. Some common types of feet include:

Dactyl: One long syllable followed by two short, – ⏑ ⏑
Spondee: Two long syllables, – –
Trochee: One long syllable followed by one short, – ⏑
Iamb: One short syllable followed by one long, ⏑ –

The common metrical patterns in Latin are:

Dactylic Hexameter: The meter of epic poetry and didactic poetry.   – ⏑ ⏑ – ⏑ ⏑ – ⏑ ⏑ – ⏑ ⏑ – ⏑ ⏑ – x

Elegiac Couplet: Used in love, elegiac, and epigrammatic poetry.
– ⏑ ⏑ – ⏑ ⏑ – ⏑ ⏑ – ⏑ ⏑ – ⏑ ⏑ – x
– ⏑ ⏑ – ⏑ ⏑ – ‖ – ⏑ ⏑ – ⏑ ⏑ –

Hendecasyllabic: Common in lyric poetry, particularly associated with Catullus. An eleven syllable line that typically starts with a spondee or a trochee, followed by a dactyl, and ends with two trochees.   x x – ⏑ ⏑ – ⏑ – ⏑ – –

Notes: When a vowel at the end of a word sees a vowel starting the next word, it drops. omne animantum becomes omn' animantum. "x" can be either short or long. ‖ is a metrical break (caesura).

Latin Poetic Meter: Dactylic Hexameter

Poetry is the magic of written words. Poems should transfix you, mesmerize you, and rhythmically transport you and your mind to new realms of thought and place. Latin got from Greek a complex system of metrical poetry. One of the most famous meters is the dactylic hexameter, in which Homer and Hesiod, the very first Greek authors, wrote their epic poems in the mid to late 700s BCE. Dactylic hexameter sounds like this:

Da ditty **da** ditty **da** ditty **da** ditty **da** ditty **da** da

If you count, you'll find six (hex) "da's" or six "longs." Longs are simply two shorts put together. It consists of six feet, where the first four can be dactyls or spondees, the fifth is usually a dactyl, and the sixth is a spondee or a trochee.

Let's look at the first lines of Vergil's *Aeneid*:

Arma virumque cano, Troiae qui primus ab oris
Italiam, fato profugus, Laviniaque venit
litora...

You can read the six parts of each line:

1.   AMRa
2.   virUMque
3.   canO
4.   TroIAE
     qui
5.   prImus
6.   ab ORis

An Approach to Translating I

Let's look at the beginning of a famous poem, *Aeneid*, written by Publius Vergilius Marc, whom we call Vergil, sometimes spelled Virgil. This is a long poem (about 63,000 words) published in 19 BCE after he died (even though he asked that the manuscript for the poem be burned).

Arma virumque cano, Troiae qui primus ab oris
Italiam, fato profugus, Laviniaque venit
litora...

How might our minds work as we translate this? Let's go in stages.

Stage 1: Literal not paying attention to endings:
Arms man-and sing, Troy who first from regions
Italy, fate exiled, Lavinian-and came
shores...

Stage 2: Paying a bit more attention to the endings:
Arms and man I sing, to/for/of Troy who first from regions
Italy, by fate exiled, and Lavinian shores he came

Stage 3: Making it better English:
I sing about arms and a man, who first from the regions of Troy to Italy, exiled by fate, he came and to the Lavinian shores

Stage 4: Making it our own:
I sing of wars and the man who was the first to come to Italy and the shores of Laviania from Troy, exile his fate.

An Approach to Translating II

Titus Lucretius Carus was born around 90 BCE and died around 50 BCE. He is famous for his epic poem (written in dactylic hexameter like Homer's *Iliad* and *Odyssey*) called the *De Rerum Natura/On the Nature of Things*. Here are the first few lines, worthy of being memorized.

> Aeneadum genetrix, hominum divomque voluptas,
> Alma Venus, caeli subter labentia signa
> quae mare navigerum, quae terras frugiferentis
> concelebras, per te quoniam genus omne animantum
> concipitur visitque exortum lumina solis ...

Stage 1: Just the word meanings
Aeneas ancestor, men gods-and desire,
Nurturing Venus, sky under slipping signs
which/who sea boat-carrying, which/who lands fruit-carrying
Celebrate, through you because kind every animated
Conceive view-and risen lights sun

Stage 2: Now paying attention to the endings
Ancestor of the descendants of Aeneas, the desire of men and of gods, Nurturing Venus, under the slipping signs of heaven, who the ship-carrying sea, who the fruit-bearing lands you celebrate, because through you every kind of thing that is alive is conceived and views the lights of the sun once risen

Stage 3: Now making it real English
Aeneas' ancestor, the desire of men and gods, dear Venus, under the stars that move through the sky, it is you who brings to life the seas that carry ships and the lands that bear the fruit, and it's through you that every living thing is conceived and once born sees the light of the sun

An Approach to Translating III

Caesar Augustus' *Res Gestae Divi Augusti* (opening)

Annos undeviginti natus exercitum privato consilio et
privata impensa comparavi, per quem rem publicam a
dominatione factionis oppressam in libertatem vindicavi.

Stage 1: Very literal word by word
Years nineteen born (one from twenty, un de viginti) army
personal plan and personal expense I put together,
through which the Republic by domination of faction
oppressed into liberty I vindicated.

The -us ending of **natus** tells us it's the subject case
The -um ending of **exercitum** tells us it's accusative
The -avi ending of **comparavi** tells us it's "I have..."
The -o endings of **privato consilio** connected through **et**
to the -a endings of **privata impensa** tell us it's either
dative or ablative
<u>**rem publicam**</u> **a dominatione factionis** <u>**oppressam**</u> is an
object sandwich typical in Latin: "the Republic,
oppressed by the domination of a faction..."

Stage 2: Now more polished
I put together an army from my own plan and my own
personal cost when I was 19, through which I liberated the
Republic, which was oppressed by the domination of a
faction.

Women Writers: Sulpicia

From Latin antiquity (outside of Christian literature), we have only one woman writer, a poet, Sulpicia. There are a few more from ancient Greece but not many and not enough. Women in antiquity no doubt wrote, but their works have not survived. Sulpicia lived around 50 BCE. This is the height of Classical Latin when Vergil and Lucretius thrived as well. Only six poems of hers survive. Here are two to enjoy.

Poem I

Tandem venit amor, qualem texisse pudori
    quam nudasse* alicui sit mihi fama magis.
Exorata meis illum Cytherea Camenis
    attulit in nostrum deposuitque sinum.
Exsolvit promissa Venus: mea gaudia narret,
    dicetur si quis non habuisse sua.
Non ego signatis quicquam mandare tabellis,
    ne legat id nemo quam meus ante, velim.
Sed peccasse iuvat, vultus componere famae
    taedet: cum digno digna fuisse ferar.

Poem II

Invisus natalis adest, qui rure molesto
    et sine Cerintho tristis agendus erit.
Dulcius urbe quid est? an villa sit apta puellae
    atque Arretino frigidus amnis agro?
Iam nimium Messalla mei studiose, quiescas,
    non tempestivae, saeve propinque, viae!
Hic animum sensusque meos abducta relinquo,
    arbitrio quamvis non sinis esse meo.

---

* nudavisse

Cicero's *In Catilinam*[1] (opening lines)

Quo usque tandem abutere, Catilina, patientia nostra?
quam diu etiam furor iste tuus nos eludet? quem ad finem
sese effrenata iactabit audacia? Nihilne te nocturnum
praesidium Palati, nihil urbis vigiliae, nihil timor populi,
nihil concursus bonorum omnium, nihil hic munitissimus
habendi senatus locus, nihil horum ora voltusque
moverunt? Patere tua consilia non sentis, constrictam iam
horum omnium scientia teneri coniurationem tuam non
vides? Quid proxima, quid superiore nocte egeris, ubi
fueris, quos convocaveris, quid consilii ceperis, quem
nostrum ignorare arbitraris? O tempora, o mores! Senatus
haec intellegit. Consul videt; hic tamen vivit. Vivit? immo
vero etiam in senatum venit, fit publici consilii particeps,
notat et designat oculis ad caedem unum quemque
nostrum. Nos autem fortes viri satis facere rei publicae
videmur, si istius furorem ac tela vitemus. Ad mortem te,
Catilina, duci iussu consulis iam pridem oportebat, in te
conferri pestem, quam tu in nos [omnes iam diu]
machinaris.

---

[1] Cicero was one of the two consuls – highest elected office – in 63 BCE when
Lucius Sergius Catalina attempted to overthrow the Roman Republic having lost the
election to consul. Cicero delivered four speeches to the Roman senate on the
attempts and these words here are the first of the first speech. These speeches, and
these opening lines, are often hailed as the finest of Latin rhetoric. You will still find
speeches today that use these Ciceronian techniques.

Caesar's *De Bello Gallico*[2] (opening lines)

Gallia est omnis divisa in partes tres, quarum unam incolunt Belgae, aliam Aquitani, tertiam qui ipsorum lingua Celtae, nostra Galli appellantur. Hi omnes lingua, institutis, legibus inter se differunt. Gallos ab Aquitanis Garumna flumen, a Belgis Matrona et Sequana dividit. Horum omnium fortissimi sunt Belgae, propterea quod a cultu atque humanitate provinciae longissime absunt, minimeque ad eos mercatores saepe commeant atque ea quae ad effeminandos animos pertinent important, proximique sunt Germanis, qui trans Rhenum incolunt, quibuscum continenter bellum gerunt. Qua de causa Helvetii quoque reliquos Gallos virtute praecedunt, quod fere cotidianis proeliis cum Germanis contendunt, cum aut suis finibus eos prohibent aut ipsi in eorum finibus bellum gerunt. Eorum una pars, quam Gallos obtinere dictum est, initium capit a flumine Rhodano, continetur Garumna flumine, Oceano, finibus Belgarum, attingit etiam ab Sequanis et Helvetiis flumen Rhenum, vergit ad septentriones. Belgae ab extremis Galliae finibus oriuntur, pertinent ad inferiorem partem fluminis Rheni, spectant in septentrionem et orientem solem. Aquitania a Garumna flumine ad Pyrenaeos montes et eam partem Oceani quae est ad Hispaniam pertinet; spectat inter occasum solis et septentriones.

---

[2] This is Gaius Julius Caesar's own account of his campaigns during the 50s BCE against the Celts and Germans in Gaul, encompassing mostly modern-day France and surrounding regions, aimed at expanding the territories of the Roman Republic. By 44 BCE, the year of his assassination, Caesar had initiated and won a civil war, establishing himself as dictator and ushering in the end of the Roman Republic.

Catullus

Poem V ad Lesbiam[3]

Vivamus mea Lesbia, atque amemus,
rumoresque senum severiorum
omnes unius aestimemus assis!
soles occidere et redire possunt:
nobis cum semel occidit brevis lux,
nox est perpetua una dormienda.
da mi basia mille, deinde centum,
dein mille altera, dein secunda centum,
deinde usque altera mille, deinde centum.
dein, cum milia multa fecerimus,
conturbabimus illa, ne sciamus,
aut ne quis malus invidere possit,
cum tantum sciat esse basiorum.

---

[3] This is the complete poem. Lesbia is the fictitious name of a real married woman
Catullus fell in love with. He wrote at the end of the Roman Republic (80s to 50s
BCE) and valued ideals of earlier Greek Hellenistic culture and writing, an era
brought on by the expansive military conquests of the Macedonian Greek general
Alexander the Great (early 300s BCE).

Vergil's *Aeneid*[4] (opening lines)

Arma virumque canō, Trōiae quī prīmus ab ōrīs
Ītaliam, fātō profugus, Lāvīniaque vēnit
lītora, multum ille et terrīs iactātus et altō
vī superum saevae memorem Iūnōnis ob īram;
multa quoque et bellō passus, dum conderet urbem,
inferretque deōs Latiō, genus unde Latīnum,
Albānīque patrēs, atque altae moenia Rōmae.

Mūsa, mihī causās memorā, quō nūmine laesō,
quidve dolēns, rēgīna deum tot volvere cāsūs
īnsīgnem pietāte virum, tot adīre labōrēs
impulerit. Tantaene animīs caelestibus īrae?

---

[4] Published after his death in 19 CE (and against his wishes), this is perhaps one the world's most famous poems, recounting the origins of Rome and by comparison, the rule of Augustus, Rome's first emperor.

Horace

Carmen XI, Liber I[5]

Tu ne quaesieris (scire nefas) quem mihi, quem tibi
finem di dederint, Leuconoe, nec Babylonios
temptaris numeros. Ut melius quicquid erit pati!
Seu pluris hiemes seu tribuit Iuppiter ultimam,
quae nunc oppositis debilitat pumicibus mare
Tyrrhenum, sapias, vina liques et spatio brevi
spem longam reseces. Dum loquimur, fugerit invida
aetas: carpe diem, quam minimum credula postero.

---

[5] This is the complete poem and where the phrase "carpe diem" originates.

Livy, *Ab Urbe Condita*[6] (opening lines)

Iam primum omnium satis constat Troia capta in ceteros
saevitum esse Troianos, duobus, Aeneae Antenorique, et
vetusti iure hospitii et quia pacis reddendaeque Helenae
semper auctores fuerant, omne ius belli Achivos
abstinuisse; casibus deinde variis Antenorem cum
multitudine Enetum, qui seditione ex Paphlagonia pulsi et
sedes et ducem rege Pylaemene ad Troiam amisso
quaerebant, venisse in intimum maris Hadriatici sinum,
Euganeisque qui inter mare Alpesque incolebant pulsis
Enetos Troianosque eas tenuisse terras. Et in quem primo
egressi sunt locum Troia vocatur pagoque inde Troiano
nomen est: gens universa Veneti appellati. Aeneam ab
simili clade domo profugum sed ad maiora rerum initia
ducentibus fatis, primo in Macedoniam venisse, inde in
Siciliam quaerentem sedes delatum, ab Sicilia classe ad
Laurentem agrum tenuisse. Troia et huic loco nomen est.

---

[6] This monumental work chronicles the fabled arrival of Aeneas from Troy to Italy
down to Augustus, Rome's first emperor. 35 of 142 books/chapters of this work
survive.

Tacitus, *Annales*[7] (opening lines)

Urbem Romam a principio reges habuere; libertatem et consulatum L. Brutus instituit. dictaturae ad tempus sumebantur; neque decemviralis potestas ultra biennium, neque tribunorum militum consulare ius diu valuit. non Cinnae, non Sullae longa dominatio; et Pompei Crassique potentia cito in Caesarem, Lepidi atque Antonii arma in Augustum cessere, qui cuncta discordiis civilibus fessa nomine principis sub imperium accepit. sed veteris populi Romani prospera vel adversa claris scriptoribus memorata sunt; temporibusque Augusti dicendis non defuere decora ingenia, donec gliscente adulatione deterrerentur. Tiberii Gaique et Claudii ac Neronis res florentibus ipsis ob metum falsae, postquam occiderant, recentibus odiis compositae sunt. inde consilium mihi pauca de Augusto et extrema tradere, mox Tiberii principatum et cetera, sine ira et studio, quorum causas procul habeo.

---

[7] The *Annals* (more accurately *Ab excessu divi Augusti*) was the last and greatest work of this Roman statesman and historian. Regrettably, we do not have all the chapters.

Ovid, *Metamorphoses*[8] (opening lines)

In nova fert animus mutatas dicere formas
corpora: di, coeptis – nam vos mutastis et illas –
adspirate meis primaque ab origine mundi
ad mea perpetuum deducite tempora carmen!

Ante mare et terras et, quod tegit omnia, caelum
unus erat toto naturae vultus in orbe,
quem dixere Chaos, rudis indigestaque moles
nec quicquam nisi pondus iners congestaque eodem
non bene iunctarum discordia semina rerum.

---

[8] Ovid wrote this just before his exile in 8 CE, during the reign of Augustus, Rome's
first emperor. This unusual epic poem of 15 books contains myths about
transformations, like Daphne whom Phoebus Apollo pursued and was turned into a
laurel tree to escape him. Greek and Roman myth often explored the complicated
relationships between the divine and human; the natural world and human-made
society and civilization.

Petronius, *Satyricon*[9] (opening lines)

Num alio genere Furiarum declamatores inquietantur, qui clamant: 'Haec vulnera pro libertate publica excepi; hunc oculum pro vobis impendi: date mihi ducem, qui me ducat ad liberos meos, nam succisi poplites membra non sustinent'? Haec ipsa tolerabilia essent, si ad eloquentiam ituris viam facerent. Nunc et rerum tumore et sententiarum vanissimo strepitu hoc tantum proficiunt ut, cum in forum venerint, putent se in alium orbem terrarum delatos. Et ideo ego adulescentulos existimo in scholis stultissimos fieri, quia nihil ex his, quae in usu habemus, aut audiunt aut vident, sed piratas cum catenis in litore stantes, sed tyrannos edicta scribentes quibus imperent filiis ut patrum suorum capita praecidant, sed responsa in pestilentiam data, ut virgines tres aut plures immolentur, sed mellitos verborum globulos, et omnia dicta factaque quasi papavere et sesamo sparsa.

---

[9] Only fragments of several chapters of this satirical novel survive. Likely written around 60 CE during the reign of Nero. Chapter 15 (practically complete) contains a dinner scene in the genre of Plato's *Symposium* called the *Cena Trimalchionis* (Trimalchio's Dinner Party).

Apuleius, *Metamorphoses*[10] (opening lines)

At ego tibi sermone isto Milesio varias fabulas conseram auresque tuas benivolas lepido susurro permulceam — modo si papyrum Aegyptiam argutia Nilotici calami inscriptam non spreveris inspicere — , figuras fortunasque hominum in alias imagines conversas et in se rursus mutuo nexu refectas ut mireris. Exordior. "Quis ille?" Paucis accipe. Hymettos Attica et Isthmos Ephyrea et Taenaros Spartiatica, glebae felices aeternum libris felicioribus conditae, mea vetus prosapia est; ibi linguam Atthidem primis pueritiae stipendiis merui. Mox in urbe Latia advena studiorum Quiritium indigenam sermonem aerumnabili labore nullo magistro praeeunte aggressus excolui. En ecce praefamur veniam, siquid exotici ac forensis sermonis rudis locutor offendero. Iam haec equidem ipsa vocis immutatio desultoriae scientiae stilo quem accessimus respondet. Fabulam Graecanicam incipimus. Lector intende: laetaberis.

---

[10] Also called *The Golden Ass*, this is the only novel in Latin to survive complete. The main character, Lucius, learns magic, turns himself into a donkey (an ass), has adventures and is eventually turned back by the goddess Isis. He might have written this later in his life around 160 CE.

Bibliography

Lockwood, D. P. *A Survey of Classical Roman Literature*, Volumes 1 and 2. The University of Chicago Press, 1962. Look for The "Midway Reprint."

Traupman, John, *The New College Latin and English Dictionary*. Bantam, 2007. The copy I have I never returned to my senior year high school Latin teacher. Sorry, Dr. Johnson.

Glare, P. G. W. (editor), *Oxford Latin Dictionary*, Oxford University Press, 1982. Reprinted with corrections 1996. My parents gave me this when I finished my PhD. This is *the* definitive Latin dictionary. It's one of the biggest books you will ever see and most expensive.

Gildersleeve, B. L. and Lodge, Gonzales, *Latin Grammar*. St Martin's Press reprint of the Third Revised Edition, MacMillan 1895. There isn't one definitive Latin grammar like there is a definitive Latin dictionary (there are several!), but this one is a good one. Yes, it's from way back when but still a standard today.

Reynolds, L. D. and Wilson, N. G., *Scribes & Scholars: A Guide to the Transmission of Greek & Latin Literature*, Third Edition, Oxford University Press 1991. Indispensable guide to the topic by superb scholars. It's technical but also highly readable. Get a copy and you'll also have a great perspective on the history of the western/European world.

Hornblower, Simon and Spawforth, Antony (editors), *The Oxford Classical Dictionary*, Third Edition, Oxford University Press, 1996. Fourth Edition is the latest. This is the standard handbook (and a big heavy one) for all things related to the classical world.

Index

200 Most Common Latin Words

(m.=masculine noun; f=feminine noun; n.=neuter noun)

Word	Definition	Part of Speech	Frequency Rank out of 200	Where to Practice in This Book
ā, ab	from, by (+ abl.)	Preposition	20	3, 46, 47, 48, 52
ac	and, and also (with comparative adjectives) than; simul ac = as soon as	Conjunction	35	45, 49, 54
accipiō, accipere, accēpī, acceptum	receive	3rd Conjugation Verb, -iō	109	49, 54
ad	to, up to, towards (+ acc.)	Preposition	13	45, 46, 48, 49, 52, 53
agō, agere, ēgī, āctum	drive, do, act	3rd Conjugation Verb, -ō	68	14, 36,44
aliquis, aliquae, aliquod	some, any si quis anyone who si quid anything that	Pronoun	76	44
alius, alia, aliud	other, another	1st and 2nd Declension Adjective	36	14, 46, 53, 54
alter, altera, alterum	other of two	1st and 2nd Declension Adjective	147	51
altus, alta, altum	high, lofty deep	1st and 2nd Declension Adjective	158	47
amīcus, amīca, amīcum	friendly (friend as noun)	1st and 2nd Declension Adjective	197	none

Word	Definition	Part of Speech	Frequency Rank out of 200	Where to Practice in This Book
amor, amōris, m.	love	3rd Declension Noun	115	44
an	or (in questions) utrum ... an = whether ... or	Conjunction	93	44
animus, animī, m.	spirit, mind	2nd Declension Noun	39	44, 46, 47, 52
annus, anni, m.	year	2nd Declension Noun	166	43
ante	before, in front of (+ acc.)	Preposition or Adverb	111	44
arma, -ōrum as plural noun, n.	arms, weapons	2nd Declension Noun	97	47, 49
at	but, but yet	Conjunction	73	54
atque	and in addition, and; after comparatives = than; simul atque, as soon as	Conjunction	34	44, 46, 47, 49, 51
audiō, audīre, audīvī/audiī, audiītum	hear, listen to	4th Conjugation Verb	164	53
aut	or	Conjunction	23	46, 51, 53
autem	moreover, but, however	Conjunction	122	45

Word	Definition	Part of Speech	Frequency Rank out of 200	Where to Practice in This Book
bellum, bellī, n.	war	2nd Declension Noun	85	46, 47, 48
beneficium, beneficiī n.	service, kindness	2nd Declension Noun	181	none
bonus, bona, bonum	good	1st and 2nd Declension Adjective	67	45
caelum, caelī, n.	sky, heavens	2nd Declension Noun	116	42, 47, 52
capiō, capere, cēpī, captum	seize	3rd Conjugation Verb, -iō	130	45, 46, 48
caput, capitis, n.	head	3rd Declension Noun	123	53
causa, causae, f.	cause, reason causā + preceding word in genitive case means for the sake of	1st Declension Noun	106	46, 47, 49
corpus, corporis, n.	body	3rd Declension Noun	74	52
crēdō, crēdere, crēdidī, crēditum	believe	3rd Conjugation Verb -ō	108	none
cum	with (prep. +abl.) when, since, although (conj. + subj.)	Preposition or Conjunction	10	44, 46, 48, 51, 53,

63

Word	Definition	Part of Speech	Frequency Rank out of 200	Where to Practice in This Book
cūra, cūrae, f.	care, concern	1st Declension Noun	185	none
dē	down from, about, concerning (+ abl.)	Preposition	45	46, 49
dēbeō, dēbēre, dēbuī, dēbitum	owe, be obliged	2nd Conjugation Verb	154	none
deinde/dein	then, next	Adverb	149	48, 51
deus, deī, m.; dea, deae, f.	god; goddess	2nd Declension Noun	41	47
dīcō, dīcere, dīxī dictum	say causam dīcere, plead a case	3rd Conjugation Verb -ō	32	44, 46, 52, 53
diēs, diēī, m. or f.	day	5th Declension Noun	53	50
dō, dare, dedī, datum	give	Verb: 1st Conjugation	27	50
dolor, dolōris, m.	pain, grief	3rd Declension Noun	192	none
domus, domūs, f.	house, home	4th Declension Noun	72	none
dūcō, dūcere, dūxī, ductum	lead, guide	3rd Conjugation Verb -ō	132	45, 48, 53

Word	Definition	Part of Speech	Frequency Rank out of 200	Where to Practice in This Book
dum	while (+ indic.) until (+ subj.) provided that (+ subj.)	Conjunction	102	47, 50
ego, meī, mihi, mē	I, me	Pronoun	11	44, 47, 49, 50, 53, 54
enim	for, indeed	Conjunction	56	none
eō, īre, iī/īvī, itum	go	Irregular Verb	96	none
ergō	therefore	Conjunction	133	none
et	and	Conjunction	1	all passages
etiam	also, even	Adverb	66	45, 46
ex, ē	out of, from (+ abl.)	Preposition	25	48, 53
faciō, facere, fēcī, factum	do, make	3rd Conjugation -iō Verb	31	45, 51, 53
fātum, fatī, n.	fate; death	2nd Declension Noun	156	47, 48
ferō, ferre, tulī, lātum	bear, carry, endure	Irregular Verb	44	52
fidēs, fideī, f.	trust, faith	5th Declension Noun	183	none
fīō, fierī, factus sum	become, happen, be done	Irregular Verb	145	53
fortūna, fortūnae, f.	fortune	1st Declension Noun	137	none

Word	Definition	Part of Speech	Frequency Rank out of 200	Where to Practice in This Book
fugiō, fugere, fūgī, fugitum	flee, escape	3rd Conjugation Verb -iō	176	50
gēns, gentis, f.	family, clan	3rd Declension Noun	193	48
genus, generis, n.	origin, lineage, kind	3rd Declension Noun	169	42, 47,
gravis, grave	heavy, serious	Adjective: 3rd Declension	139	none
habeō, habēre, habuī, habitum	have, hold	2nd Conjugation Verb	38	44, 45, 49, 53
hīc	here; hinc: from here	Adverb	79	44, 45
hic, haec, hoc	this, these	Pronoun	7	45, 53, 54
homō, hominis, m.	human being	3rd Declension Noun	87	42, 54
hostis, hostis, m. or f.	stranger, enemy	3rd Declension Noun	92	none
iam	now; already	Adverb	33	44, 45, 48, 54
īdem, eadem, idem	the same	Pronoun	58	none

Word	Definition	Part of Speech	Frequency Rank out of 200	Where to Practice in This Book
ignis, ignis, m.	fire	3rd Declension Noun	150	none
ille, illa, illud	that	Pronoun	8	44, 47, 51, 52, 54
imperium, imperiī, n.	command, power	2nd Declension Noun	199	49
in	in, on (+ abl.); into, onto (+ acc.)	Preposition	5	44, 45, 46, 48, 49, 52, 53, 54
inquam, inquis, inquit, inquiunt	say (used with direct speech)	Irregular Verb	162	none
inter	between, among; during (+ acc.)	Preposition	63	46, 48
ipse, ipsa, ipsum	himself, herself, itself	Pronoun	21	46, 49, 53, 54
īra, irae, f.	wrath, anger	1st Declension Noun	186	47, 49
is, ea, id	he, she, it	Pronoun	12	44, 46
iste, ista, istud	that, that of yours; adverb istīc or istūc: over there; istinc: from over there	Pronoun	80	45
iubeō, iubēre, iussī, iussum	order	2nd Conjugation Verb	83	45

Word	Definition	Part of Speech	Frequency Rank out of 200	Where to Practice in This Book
labor, labōris, m.	work, effort	3rd Declension Noun	200	47, 54
licet, licēre, licuit, licitum est	it is permitted (+ dat. + infinitive "it is permitted for someone/something to do...")	Verb: Impersonal	174	none
locus, locī, m.	place; loca (neuter plural) region	2nd Declension Noun	61	45, 48
longus, longa, longum	long, far	1st and 2nd Declension Adjective	141	46, 49, 50
magis	more	Adverb	89	44
māgnus, mānga, māgnum	great	1st and 2nd Declension Adjective	24	14
manus, manūs, f.	hand; band of men	4th Declension Noun	47	none
mare, maris, n.	sea	3rd Declension Noun	124	42, 48, 50, 52
māter, mātris, f.	mother	3rd Declension Noun	126	none

Word	Definition	Part of Speech	Frequency Rank out of 200	Where to Practice in This Book
medius, media, medium	middle, central	1st and 2nd Declension Adjective	161	none
mēns, mentis, f.	mind	3rd Declension Noun	172	none
meus, mea meum	my	Pronoun	40	44, 51, 52, 54
mīles, mīlitis, m.	soldier	3rd Declension Noun	160	49
miser, misera, miserum	wretched, pitiable	1st and 2nd Declension Adjective	136	none
mittō, mittere, mīsī, missum	send, let go	3rd Conjugation Verb -ō	113	none
modo	only, merely; modo ... modo: now ... now, sometimes ... sometimes	Adverb	151	54
modus, modī, m.	measure, manner, kind	2nd Declension Noun	194	none
mors, mortis, f.	death	3rd Declension Noun	94	45
mōs, mōris, m.	custom, habit; (pl.) character	3rd Declension Noun	180	45

Word	Definition	Part of Speech	Frequency Rank out of 200	Where to Practice in This Book
moveō, movēre, mōvī, mōtum	move	2nd Conjugation Verb	191	45
multus, multa, multum	much, many; multō, by far	1st and 2nd Declension Adjective	42	47, 51
nam or namque	for, indeed, really	Conjunction	60	52, 53
nātūra, -nātūrae, f.	nature	1st Declension Noun	179	52
nē	that not (in order that something not happen)	Conjunction	46	44, 50, 51
nec	and not, nor; nec ... nec, neither ... nor	Conjunction	18	50, 52
nēmō	no one (gen. nūllīus, dat. nūllī, abl. nūllō or nūllā)	Pronoun	178	44
neque	and not, nor; neque ... neque, neither ... nor	Conjunction	71	49
nihil, nīl	nothing; not at all	Noun: Indeclinable	54	14, 45, 53
nisi, nī	if not, unless	Conjunction	99	52
nōmen, nōminis, n.	name	3rd Declension Noun	134	48, 49
nōn	not	Adverb	6	44, 45, 49, 52, 53, 54

Word	Definition	Part of Speech	Frequency Rank out of 200	Where to Practice in This Book
nōs, nostrum or nostrī, nōbīs, nōs	we	Pronoun	50	44, 45, 46
noster, nostra, nostrum	our	Pronoun	51	45, 46
novus, nova, novum	new	1st and 2nd Declension Adjective	138	52
nox, noctis, f.	night	3rd Declension Noun	118	45, 51
nūllus, nūlla, nūllum	not any, no one	1st and 2nd Declension Adjective	48	54
nunc	now	Adverb	49	50, 53
omnis, omne	all, every, as a whole	Adjective: 3rd Declension	17	42, 45, 46, 48, 51
ōs, ōris, n.	mouth, face	3rd Declension Noun	146	47
parēns, pārentis, m. or f.	parent	3rd Declension Noun	189	none
parō, parāre	prepare, acquire	Verb: 1st Conjugation	159	none
pars, partis, f.	part	3rd Declension Noun	64	14, 46

Word	Definition	Part of Speech	Frequency Rank out of 200	Where to Practice in This Book
parvus, parva, parvum	small	1st and 2nd Declension Adjective	142	none
pater, patris, m.	father, ancestor	3rd Declension Noun	70	45, 47, 53
patior, patī, passus sum	experience, undergo	Verb: Deponent	184	47, 50
pectus, pectoris, n.	chest, breast	3rd Declension Noun	182	none
per	through (+ acc.)	Preposition	29	14, 42, 43,
pēs, pedis, m.	foot	3rd Declension Noun	198	none
petō, petere, petīvī, petītum	seek, aim at	3rd Conjugation Verb -ō	82	none
pōnō, pōnere, posuī, positum	put, place; put aside	3rd Conjugation Verb -ō	101	none
populus, populī, m.	people	2nd Declension Noun	121	45, 49
possum, posse, potuī	be able	Irregular Verb	22	51
post	after (adv. or prep. + acc.)	Preposition or Adverb	163	none

DICTIONARY

Word	Definition	Part of Speech	Frequency Rank out of 200	Where to Practice in This Book
prīmus, prima, primum	first	1st and 2nd Declension Adjective	90	47, 48, 52, 54
prō	for, on behalf of, in proportion to (+ abl.)	Preposition	127	53
prope	near, next; (comp.) propior, (superl.) proximus; (adverb) prope, nearly, almost	Preposition	188	none
puer, puerī, m.	boy; slave	2nd Declension Noun	190	none but see 44 and 54
putō, putāre	think, suppose	Verb: 1st Conjugation	165	53
quaerō, quaerere, quesīvī, quaesītum	seek, inquire	3rd Conjugation Verb -ō	112	48, 50
quam	how? (after comparative) than	Adverb	28	44, 45, 46, 50
-que	and (attached to end of word)	Conjunction	4	47, 51, 52, 53, 54
quī, quae, quod	who, which, what	Pronoun	3	42, 46, 50, 52, 53
quia	because	Conjunction	131	48, 53
quīdam, quaedam, quoddam,	a certain one, someone	Pronoun	125	14
quidem	certainly, at least	Adverb	135	none

Word	Definition	Part of Speech	Frequency Rank out of 200	Where to Practice in This Book
quisque, quaeque, quidque	each one, everyone	Pronoun	196	none
quisquis, quidquid	whoever, whichever	Pronoun	128	none
quoque	also, too	Conjunction	75	46, 47,
reddō, reddere reddidī redditum	return, give back	3rd Conjugation Verb -ō	173	48
referō referre, rettulī, relātum	bring back; report	Irregular Verb	170	none
rēgnum, rēgnī, n.	kingship, kingdom	2nd Declension Noun	120	none
relinquō, relinquere, relīquī, relictum	abandon	3rd Conjugation Verb -ō	143	44
rēs, reī, f.	thing (rēs pūblica, commonwealth, republic)	5th Declension Noun	37	43, 49
rēx, rēgis, m.	king	3rd Declension Noun	59	48, 49
saepe	often	Adverb	144	46

Word	Definition	Part of Speech	Frequency Rank out of 200	Where to Practice in This Book
scelus, sceleris, n.	crime, sin	3rd Declension Noun	153	none
sciō, scīre, scīvī/sciī, scītum	know	4th Conjugation Verb	171	50, 51
sed	but	Conjunction	19	44, 48, 49, 53
semper	always, ever	Adverb	148	48
sequor, sequī, secūtus sum	follow	Verb: Deponent	107	none
sī	if	Conjunction	15	14, 44, 45, 53, 54
sīc	thus, so, in this way; sīc ... ut: in the same way as	Adverb	78	14
sine	without (+ abl.)	Preposition	103	44, 49
sōlus, sōla, sōlum	only, alone	1st and 2nd Declension Adjective	175	none
stō, stāre, stetī, statum	stand	1st Conjugation Verb	167	none
sub	under, close to (+ acc. or abl.)	Preposition	117	49
sui, sibi, sē/sēsē	himself, herself, itself, themselves	Pronoun	16	46, 53

DICTIONARY

Word	Definition	Part of Speech	Frequency Rank out of 200	Where to Practice in This Book
sum, esse, fuī, futūrum	be, exist; fut. infinitive. often = fore, impf. subj. often = forem for essem	Irregular Verb	2	44, 48, 49 51
superus, supera, superum	situated above, upper	1st and 2nd Declension Adjective	98	45, 47
suus, sua, suum	his own, her own, its own	1st and 2nd Declension Adjective	26	44
tam	so, so much	Adverb	95	none
tamen	nevertheless, still	Conjunction	57	14, 45
tantus, tanta, tantum	so great, so much; such a quantity	1st and 2nd Declension Adjective	104	47, 51, 53
tempus, temporis, n.	time	3rd Declension Noun	88	45, 49, 52
teneō, tenēre, tenuī, tentum	hold, keep	2nd Conjugation Verb	105	45
terra, terrae, f.	land	1st Declension Noun	69	42, 47, 48, 52, 53
timeō, timēre, timuī	to fear, to dread	2nd Conjugation Verb	152	none
tōtus, tōta, tōum	whole, entire	1st and 2nd Declension Adjective	77	52

Word	Definition	Part of Speech	Frequency Rank out of 200	Where to Practice in This Book
tū, tuī, tibi tē	you (singular)	Pronoun	9	14, 45, 50, 54
tum or tunc	then	Adverb	55	none
tuus, tua, tuum	your	1st and 2nd Declension Adjective	43	45, 54
ubi	where, when	Adverb	91	45
ūllus, ūlla, ūllum	any, anyone	1st and 2nd Declension Adjective	177	none
ūnus, ūna, ūnum	one	1st and 2nd Declension Adjective	52	45, 52
urbs, urbis, f.	city	3rd Declension Noun	81	44, 45, 47, 49, 54
ut, utī	as (+ indic.); so that (+ subj.); (in questions) in what manner, how	Adverb	14	50, 53, 54
vel	even (adv.); or (conj.) vel ... vel: either ... or	Adverb or Conjunction	140	49
veniō, venīre, vēnī, ventum	come	4th Conjugation Verb	62	44, 45, 47, 48, 54
verbum, verbī, n.	word	2nd Declension Noun	187	53
via, viae, f.	way, street	1st Declension Noun	195	44, 53

DICTIONARY

Word	Definition	Part of Speech	Frequency Rank out of 200	Where to Practice in This Book
videō, vidēre, vīdī, vīsum	see	2nd Conjugation Verb	30	45, 53
vincō, vincere, vīcī, victum	conquer	3rd Conjugation Verb -ō	100	none
vir, virī, m.	man	2nd Declension Noun	84	45, 47
virtūs, virtūtis, f.	virtue, manliness	3rd Declension Noun	110	46
vīs, (no gen.), f.	force; vim (acc.), vī (abl.); vīrēs (pl.), strength	3rd Declension Noun	114	none
vīta, vitae, f.	life	1st Declension Noun	86	14, 45
vīvō, vīvere. vīxī, victum	live	3rd Conjugation Verb -ō	155	45, 51
vocō, vocāre	call	1st Conjugation Verb	157	48
volō, velle, voluī	wish, be willing	Irregular Verb	65	14

Word	Definition	Part of Speech	Frequency Rank out of 200	Where to Practice in This Book
vōs	you (pl.); (gen.) vestrum/vestrī, (dat./abl.) vōbīs, (acc.) vōs	1st and 2nd Declension Adjective	129	52
vōx, vōcis, f.	voice, sound, word	3rd Declension Noun	168	54